Have you seen Josephine?

Stéphane Poulin

Tundra Books

My name is Daniel and I live near a bridge in Montreal.
My cat's name is Josephine.
She lives with my father and me.

Everybody knows Josephine.
When she is with me, people ask: "How is Josephine today?"
When she is not with me, they ask: "Where is Josephine today?"
I always know the answer. Unless it is Saturday.

Where does Josephine go on Saturday?

Last Saturday I decided to find out.

I woke up very early, just in time to see her leave my room.
"Where are you going, Josephine?" I called to her.
"Brupp," she said, and disappeared into the basement.

She plays games with me.
She likes me to follow her.
Then as soon as I get close enough to grab her, she runs off.

Or she likes to watch me looking for her.
She sits still and waits until I see her.
Then she moves off again.

I looked into the basement.
"Are you there, Josephine?" I called.

Not a sound.
It was too dark to see.
I was too scared to go down.

But it wouldn't help, anyway.
She uses the basement window to go
　　in and out of the house.
If I went down she would just run out
　　into the back lane.

I went out to look for her.

A garbage truck was passing by.
"Have you seen Josephine?" I asked the man.
"I haven't seen any little girls this morning," he said.

He was a new garbage man.

"Josephine is a cat," I told him. "My cat."
"I've seen lots of cats," he said.
"Josephine is the color of vanilla ice cream, with black paws,
    black ears and black around her eyes."
"I haven't seen any vanilla and chocolate cats this morning,"
    he said and moved off.

I looked under the steps where she likes to hide.
She wasn't there.

My father was hanging out clothes.
"Will you help me find Josephine?" I asked him.
"Sure," he said. "Where do you want to look?"
"If we go up on the bridge maybe we can see her."
"Let's go," he said.

I like looking down from the bridge.
We often walk up there, even when I'm not looking for Josephine.
We can see everything everywhere, all the streets and houses.
Even the roof of our own house.

"I see her, I see her." I pointed. Josephine looked up as if she heard me. Then she ran around a corner.

"I know where she's going," I said. "To Clara's for ice cream." "Let's go then," said my father.

Josephine must have waited for us.
When we turned the corner onto Clara's street,
  she was right there.
She jumped and ran off fast.
A woman was so scared
  she dropped her ice-cream cone.

"What are you doing, Josephine?"
  Clara called to her.
But Josephine went right by the store.

"I've run enough for one morning,"
  my father said.
"I'll wait for you at home."

Josephine ran on down the street to the fish store.

The fish man likes cats and Josephine likes him.
"Did you see Josephine?" I asked him.

He doesn't speak like me and I don't know how to speak like him.
But he understood. He pointed down an alleyway.
I was just in time to see Josephine's tail disappear.

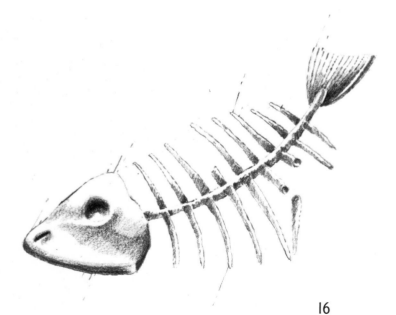

I went around to the playground.

"Have you seen Josephine?" I asked my friend Christiane.
"She was here a minute ago," Christiane said.

I looked around and then I saw her.
She was sitting on the fence watching me.
"I see you!"
As soon as I said it, she jumped down and ran towards home.

I followed her.

She ran just fast enough to keep a little ahead of me.
I saw her turn into our yard.

I was glad to get home.
"Where's Josephine?" I asked my father.
"I haven't seen her," he said.
"But I saw her come in here," I said.

"Listen!" My father held up his hand. "I hear something."
"It's coming from the Gagnon yard."

I was just in time to see Josephine go through a hole
   in the Gagnon fence.
The Gagnons used to have a restaurant near us,
   but now they stay home.

I climbed up and looked over.

And there was Josephine. With more cats than I could count.

"What are you doing there, Josephine?" I called to her.
She looked up at me and said, "Brupp."
This time she didn't run off.
She waited while Mrs. Gagnon gave her a dish of food.

"Hello, Daniel." Mrs. Gagnon called to me.
"Do you like our cat party? We have one every Saturday."

"Yes," I said, and tried again to count the cats.

"Would you like to help serve?" Mr. Gagnon asked me.
"We need another waiter."

"I'll ask my father," I said.

And I did.

To Françoise, my mother whom I love

© 1986, Stéphane Poulin

ISBN 0-88776-180-1 hardcover 10, 9, 8, 7, 6, 5, 4, 3, 2
ISBN 0-88776-215-8 paperback 10, 9, 8, 7, 6, 5, 4, 3, 2, 1

Published in Canada by Tundra Books, Montreal, Quebec H3G 1R4 ISBN 0-88776-180-1

Published in the United States by Tundra Books of Northern New York, Plattsburgh, N.Y. 12901

Canadian Cataloguing in Publication Data: Poulin, Stéphane, 1961 – . Have you seen Josephine? ISBN 0-88776-180-1 1. Poulin, Stéphane. 2. Montréal (Québec) in art. I. Title   ND249.P68A4 1986 759.11   C86-090101-7

Printed in Belgium